MW01357535

COLORING BOOK TO

- - - - - - - - - -

- - - - - - - - -

WUBBA LUBBA

DUB DUB!

WUBBA LUBBA

DUB DUB!

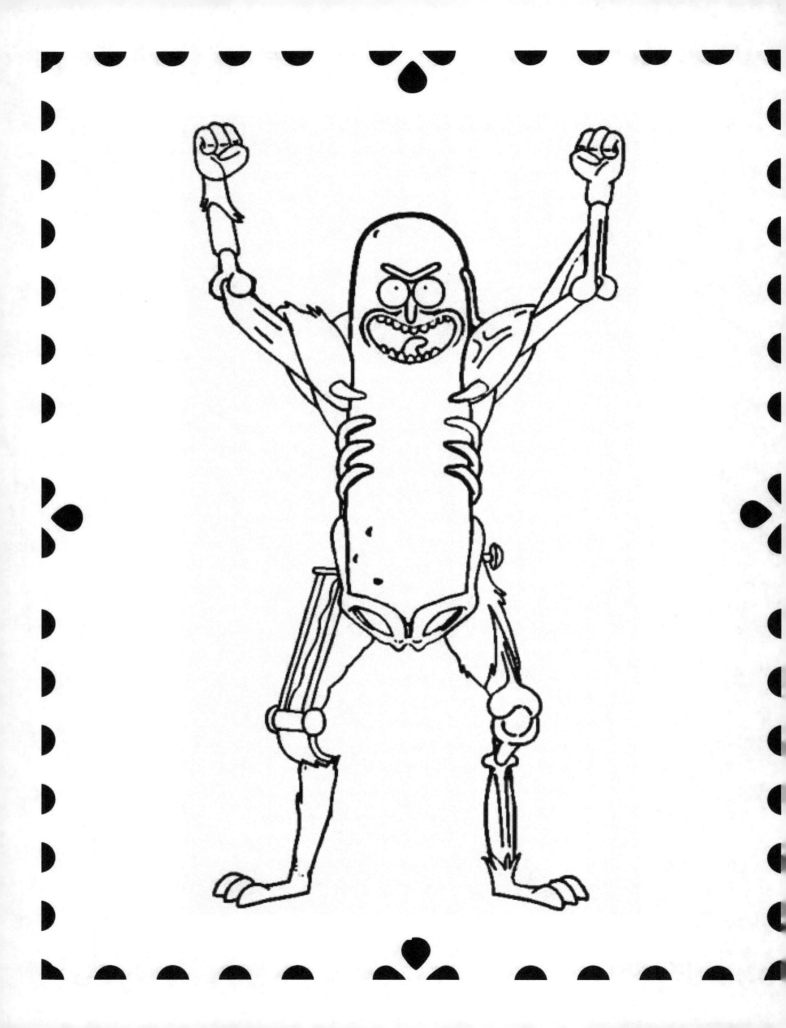

Peace among Worlds

Rick and Morty

DRAW HERE WHAT YOU LEARNED

DRAW HERE WHAT YOU LEARNED

DRAW HERE WHAT YOU LEARNED

DRAW HERE WHAT YOU LEARNED

DRAW HERE WHAT YOU LEARNED

DRAW HERE WHAT YOU LEARNED

DRAW HERE WHAT YOU LEARNED

DRAW HERE WHAT YOU LEARNED

DRAW HERE WHAT YOU LEARNED

DRAW HERE WHAT YOU LEARNED

DRAW HERE WHAT YOU LEARNED

DRAW HERE WHAT YOU LEARNED

DRAW HERE WHAT YOU LEARNED

DRAW HERE WHAT YOU LEARNED

DRAW HERE WHAT YOU LEARNED

DRAW HERE WHAT YOU LEARNED

DRAW HERE WHAT YOU LEARNED

DRAW HERE WHAT YOU LEARNED

Printed in the USA
CPSIA information can be obtained
at www.ICGtesting.com
LVHW081736031224
798225LV00017B/1485